SPIDERS

by Liza Jacobs

BLACKBIRCH®
PRESS

THOMSON

━━━━━━✦━━━━━━ ™

GALE

San Diego • Detroit • New York • San Francisco • Cleveland • New Haven, Conn. • Waterville, Maine • London • Munich

For more information, contact
The Gale Group, Inc.
27500 Drake Rd.
Farmington Hills, MI 48331-3535
Or you can visit our Internet site at http://www.gale.com

No. 274-1, Sec.1 Ho-Ping E. Rd., Taipei, Taiwan, R.O.C.
Tel: 886-2-2363-3486 Fax: 886-2-2363-6081

LIBRARY OF CONGRESS CATALOGING-IN-PUBLICATION DATA

Jacobs,Liza.
  Spiders / By Liza Jacobs.
    v. cm. — (Wild Wild World)
  Includes bibliographical references and index.
  Contents: About spiders — Web- builders — Egg laying.
   ISBN 1-4103-0044-7 (hardback : alk. paper)

  1. Spiders—Juvenile literature. [1. Spiders.] I. Title II. Series.

  QL458.4.J36 2003
  595.4'4—dc21

                                          2003005145

Printed in Taiwan
10 9 8 7 6 5 4 3 2 1

Table of Contents

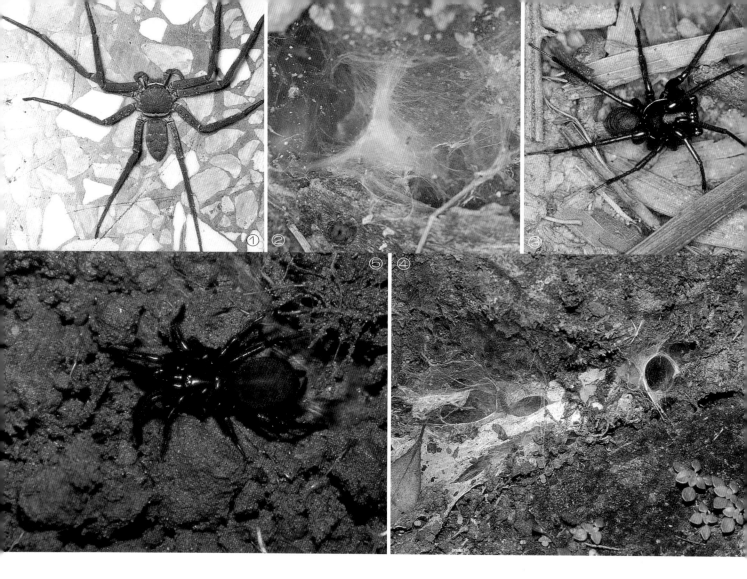

About Spiders

There are more than 40,000 different kinds of spiders! Many people think spiders are insects, but they are not. Spiders are arachnids. Insects have 6 legs. All spiders have 8 legs and make silk.

Some spiders build webs with their silk. Others spin long silk threads to jump from one place to another. These spiders are often called jumping spiders. Jumping spiders burrow into holes in the ground, rocks, or tree trunks.

They find shelter in leaves, branches, and on the water's surface.

Many jumping spiders protect their homes by covering the entrances with silk.

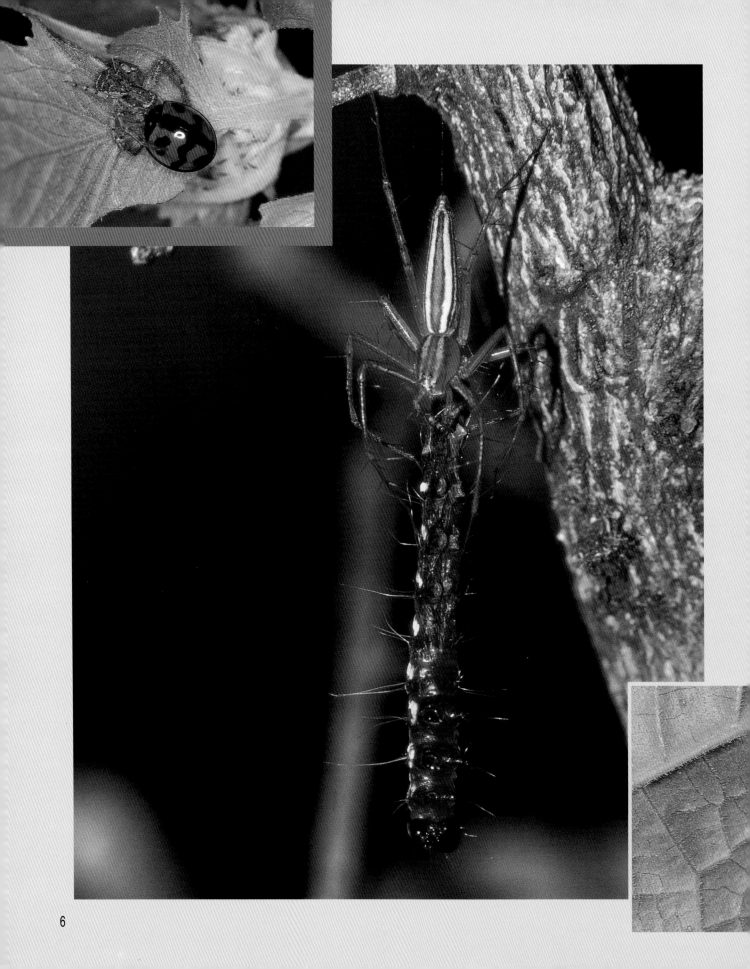

Drinking Food

Since jumping spiders do not spin webs, they need other ways to catch food. Unlike most kinds of spiders, they have sharp eyesight. They also move quietly and jump very fast.

A jumping spider waits silently until its prey (animal hunted for food) wanders nearby. Then it pounces on it! The victim is then wrapped tightly in the spider's silk so it can't get away. Many spiders also bite their prey. The bite injects poison that either kills the prey or makes it unable to move.

Spiders can't chew or swallow, so they need to drink their food. They shoot digestive fluid into their prey that softens their meal and makes it ready to drink!

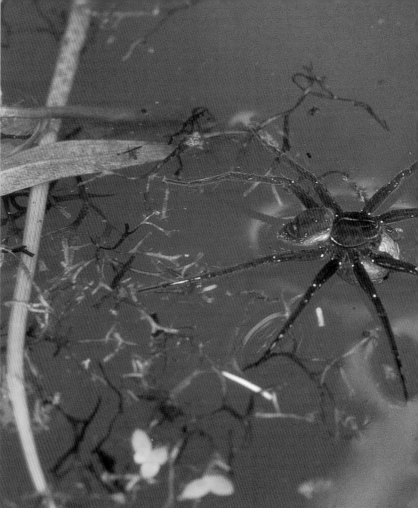

Mating

Male jumping spiders often do a kind of dance to attract a female. After mating, female jumping spiders lay their eggs and protect them with an egg sac made of silk.

Many females carry the egg sac with them until the babies are ready to hatch. The female also uses her silk to attach the egg sac to her body. Other female jumping spiders lay their egg sacs on plants or in leaf litter.

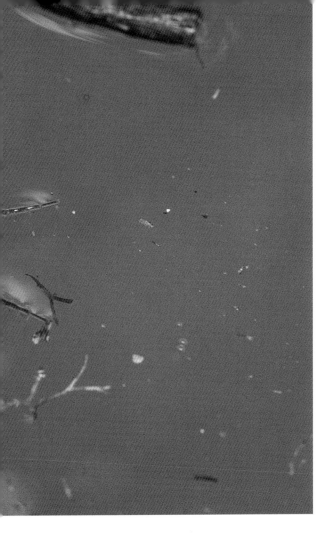

When the eggs hatch,
hundreds of spiders come
scrambling out. Many
jumping spiders carry
their babies around on
their backs until they are
ready to live on their own.

Incredible Jumpers

There are thousands of different kinds of jumping spiders. They live in many parts of the world and are found in a wide variety of colors and sizes. Jumping spiders are amazing—they can jump more than 25 times their own body length!

11

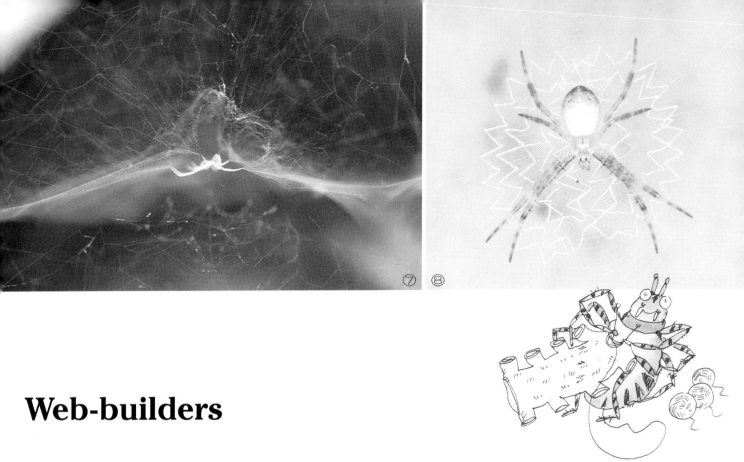

⑦ ⑧

Web-builders

Like jumping spiders, web-building spiders also use their
silk to travel safely from one place to another. These spiders
weave webs in all kinds of shapes and sizes. Spiders make
beautiful webs shaped like baskets, cradles, tents, orbs,
spirals, and even flowers. There are also irregular-shaped
webs and webs that have thick X-shaped sections.

⑨ ⑩

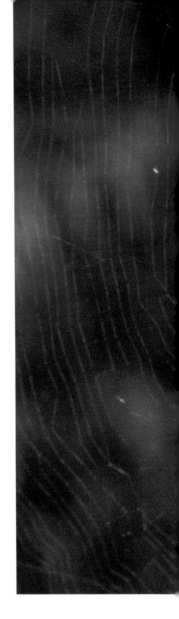

Working the Web

Spiders make silk with special body parts on their abdomens called spinnerets. Web-making spiders spend hours using their silk to build and fix their webs.

A spider uses its web to catch prey. Most spiders have 8 eyes, but do not have very good eyesight. They do have sensory organs called pedipalps on either side of their jaw and fine hairs on their legs that help them feel when something moves nearby.

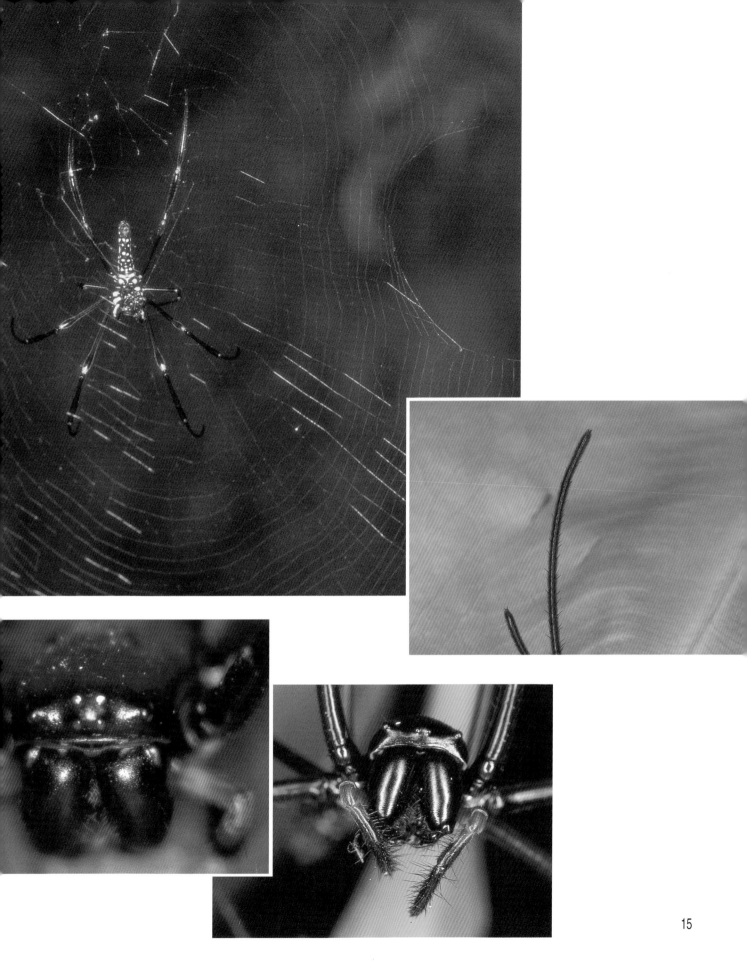

Tricky Traps

Some webs are sticky, some are tightly woven, and others are loose. But all webs have one thing in common—they trap most insects that fly or wander into them.

After their prey is caught, some spiders also spin thread to wrap up their meal. Many spiders also bite their prey, sending liquid poison into them. This either kills the insect or makes it unable to move. Either way, the prey is ready to be turned to liquid with digestive fluid and sucked up by the spider!

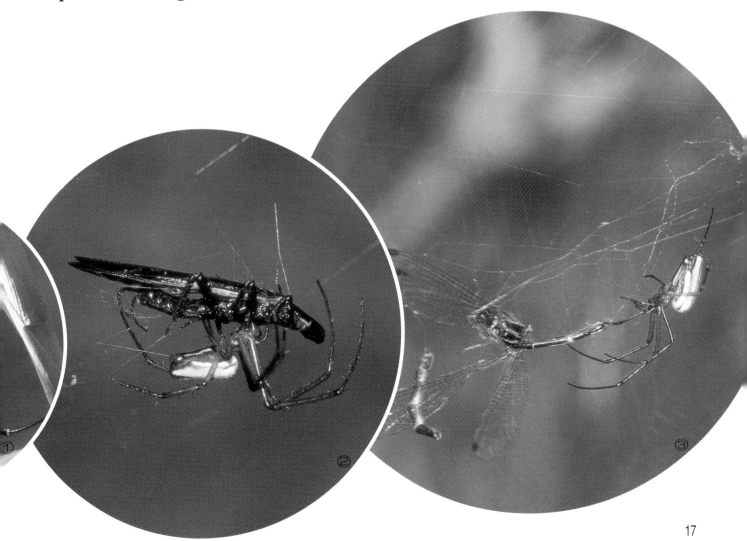

Egg Laying

When spiders are ready to mate, males often do a dance to attract females. After mating, baby spiders begin to develop.

When female spiders lay their eggs, most spin silk to make a covering around them. This egg sac protects the spider's eggs. Many spiders also use their silk to safely attach an egg sac to a leaf or branch. Some mothers leave the sac and do not return, while others stay nearby to guard their eggs.

Spiderlings

Baby spiders are called spiderlings. They have sharp edges on their pedipalps called egg teeth. When the babies are ready to hatch, they use their egg teeth to break through their shell. They swarm out of the egg sac, often by the hundreds. Many kinds of baby spiders are able to make silk thread right away. They can be seen spinning and dangling from their threads as they make their way to safety.

Thousands of Webs

There are thousands of different kinds of spiders that build webs. These webs serve as a spider's home and are also used to catch prey. Spiders live all over the world and weave webs in many beautiful shapes and sizes.

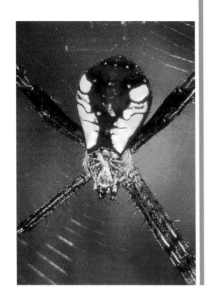

For More Information

Facklam, Margery. *Spiders and Their Web Sites*. New York: Little, Brown and Company, 2001.

Markle, Sandra. *Outside and Inside Spiders*. New York: Scholastic, 1994.

Stefoff, Rebecca. *Spider*. New York: Marshall Cavendish, 1999.

Glossary

pedipalps leg-like parts near a spider's mouth

prey an animal that is hunted for food

spiderling baby spider

spinnerets openings on a spider's abdomen through which silk is spun